Shockingly Silly Jokes About Electricity and Magnetism

Laugh and Learn About Science

Written by Melissa Stewart
Illustrated by Gerald Kelley

Enslow Elementary, an imprint of Enslow Publishers, Inc.

Enslow Elementary is a registered trademark of Enslow Publishers, Inc.

Library of Congress Cataloging-in-Publication Data:
Stewart, Melissa.
  Shockingly silly jokes about electricity and magnetism : laugh and learn about science / written by Melissa Stewart ; illustrated by Gerald Kelley.
      p. cm. — (Super silly science jokes)
  Includes index.
  Summary: "Learn about electricity, static, magnetism, and more. Read jokes about all of these topics, and learn how to write your own"— Provided by publisher.
  ISBN 978-0-7660-3967-4
  1. Electricity—Juvenile literature. 2. Magnetism—Juvenile literature. 3. Electricity—Juvenile humor. 4. Magnetism—Juvenile humor. I. Kelley, Gerald, ill. II. Title.
  QC527.2.S74 2013
  537—dc23

                                2011026530

Future editions:
Paperback ISBN 978-1-4644-0163-3
ePUB ISBN 978-1-4645-1070-0
PDF ISBN 978-1-4645-1070-7

Printed in China

012012 Leo Paper Group, Heshan City, Guangdong, China

10 9 8 7 6 5 4 3 2 1

To Our Readers: We have done our best to make sure all Internet Addresses in this book were active and appropriate when we went to press. However, the author and the publisher have no control over and assume no liability for the material available on those Internet sites or on other Web sites they may link to. Any comments or suggestions can be sent by e-mail to comments@enslow.com or to the address on the back cover.

Illustration Credits: © 2011 Gerald Kelley (www.geraldkelley.com)

Photo Credits: © 2011 Photos.com, a division of Getty Images, pp. 8, 11, 13, 20, 36; Alamy: © giantdog, p. 19, © WaterFram, p. 4; Dayna N Mason, www.flickr.com/photos/daynoir, p. 24; Enslow Publishers, Inc., p. 44; © iStockphoto.com/Chris Price, p. 35; Photo Researchers, Inc.: GIPhotoStock, p. 31, Joel Arem, p. 23, Spencer Grant, p. 32; Shutterstock.com, pp. 1, 7, 14, 16, 27, 28, 38, 40, 43.

Cover Illustration: © 2011 Gerald Kelley (www.geraldkelley.com)

Enslow Elementary
an imprint of

Enslow Publishers, Inc.
40 Industrial Road
Box 398
Berkeley Heights, NJ 07922
USA
        http://www.enslow.com

Contents

It's Natural!

Electric stingrays. Electric eels. Electric catfish.

What do these three fish have in common? They all **stun** their supper—and their enemies—with high-powered pulses of energy. And they aren't alone. At least a hundred kinds of animals zap predators and prey with **electricity**.

Natural electricity also causes the gentle jolt you feel when you shuffle across a carpet and touch a doorknob. It makes the crackling sound you hear when you take off a sweater. It even triggers the bright **lightning** flashes you see during summer storms.

As you read this book, you'll learn lots more about electricity, and **magnetism** too. But that's not all. This book is also chock full of jokes. Some of them will make you laugh out loud. Other might make you groan. (Sorry.) But either way, you'll have a good time. So let's get started!

2 Inside an Atom

Have you ever heard anyone talk about natural electricity before? If not, that's no surprise. Most people call it "**static electricity**." It's the buildup of electric charges on an object.

What does that mean? Let's look inside an **atom**.

Everything in the world is made of tiny atoms. And atoms are made up of three smaller particles. They are called **protons**, **neutrons**, and **electrons**.

Protons have a positive electric charge. Neutrons have no charge. And electrons have a negative electric charge. Atoms have the same number of protons and electrons, so their charges balance out.

But sometimes electrons get pulled off an atom. And that's when things get interesting. Want to know why? Turn the page.

Q: Why did the proton look on the bright side?

A: Because it always stays positive.

Q: What did the ticket seller at the movie theater say to the atomic particle?

A: "No charge for neutrons."

Protons and neutrons make up the center, or nucleus, of an atom. Electrons are always on the move. They whiz around the nucleus.

3 What a Shock!

What happens when you shuffle across a carpet and touch a doorknob? You feel a gentle jolt. If it's dark, you might even see a small spark.

What causes that shock? Moving electrons.

As you scuff your feet on the rug, negatively charged electrons get pulled off the atoms that make up the rug. And those electrons become part of the atoms on the surface of your body.

With each step, more and more negative electric charges build up on your skin. By the time you reach the door, your body is covered with static electricity.

When you touch the doorknob, ZAP! You feel a shock as a stream of electrons jumps from the atoms on your hand to the atoms on the surface of the doorknob.

Q: What do electrons wear on their feet?

A: Anti-shock socks.

Q: How does static electricity tell time?

A: With a shock clock.

It's Static, Not Magic

4

The word *electric* comes from the Latin term *electrum*. It means "amber." What does amber—fossilized tree **resin**—have to do with charged particles? More than you might think.

About 2,600 years ago a Greek thinker named Thales made a surprising discovery. When he rubbed amber against a piece of cloth, bits of straw stuck to the amber.

Was it magic? No way! Thales didn't know it, but he was seeing static electricity in action.

Around 1600, British scientist William Gilbert experimented with amber and other "electrics"—materials that easily build up a charge. Thanks to his work, German scientist Otto von Guerike invented a machine that could produce static electricity. By the late 1600s, people called electricians were using these friction machines to perform some amazing tricks.

What kind of tricks? Turn the page to find out.

Q: What do "amber" and "straw" have in common?

A: Both words have five letters.

This piece of amber formed millions of years ago.

Q: What did the electron do on April Fool's Day?

A: She played an elec-trick on her brother.

5

Making Sparks Fly

As an electrician spun a friction machine's crank, a charge built up on a glass tube. When the electrician placed a metal rod close to the glass tube, sparks flew. And if a volunteer held a finger close to the glass tube, ZAP!

Sometimes an electrician used silk cords to hoist a boy into the air. When the electrician rubbed the boy's feet with an electrically charged glass tube, sparks shot out of the boy's hands and face. Yikes!

Around 1734, Georg Matthias Bose, a German scientist, hosted a shocking dinner party. As his guests ate, he touched a charged glass rod to the table. Sparks danced between the table and the guests' forks. Pretty cool, huh?

Q: Where did Georg Matthias Bose buy his glass rods?

A: At the shocking mall.

Q: Where do electrons go to have fun?

A: The spark park.

The Key and the Kite

When Benjamin Franklin saw an electrician perform, he wanted to get in on the fun. So he started experimenting with electricity. Then a revolutionary idea struck him. Maybe zigzagging lightning bolts were the same as the small sparks he was creating in his workshop. Maybe lightning was triggered by static electricity.

Bet you know what Ben did next. That's right. He risked his life.

Flying a kite in a thunderstorm is a BAD idea. But Ben did it anyway. When he saw loose threads on his kite string pop straight up, he got excited. So he moved his hand toward the key. ZAP! Ben felt a shock. And he saw a bright spark. That's when Ben knew he was right.

Q: Why did Benjamin Franklin fly a kite in 1752?

A: The idea that lightning was a giant electric spark had him all charged up.

Q: How did scientists react to Ben Franklin's discovery?

A: They were shocked.

A Look at Lightning

Why does lightning strike? To find out, let's look inside a thundercloud.

Chilly air freezes tiny water droplets into icy bits. Then swirling winds toss the ice around.

CRASH! BOOM! BAM! Electrons get knocked off the smaller slivers. They stick to the larger bits of ice. That makes the larger pieces negatively charged. And the smaller slivers become positively charged.

The larger, heavier pieces fall. But air currents lift the smaller, lighter pieces up. Soon, the top of the cloud is positively charged. And the bottom is negatively charged.

What happens next? Negative charges attract positive charges. That means the ground below the thunderhead becomes positively charged. When the difference between the positive charges on the ground and the negative charges in the cloud is great enough, LOOK OUT! A sizzling stream of electricity bursts out of the cloud and plunges downward.

Q: Why did the scientist decide to study lightning?

A: It struck his fancy.

Q: Why do raindrops like lightning at night?

A: It helps them see where they're going.

17

Packets of Power

A lemon. A nail. A penny. Insulated wire. Put them together and what do you get? Power.

Here's how: Cut two pieces of wire and strip the insulation off the ends. Wrap one piece of wire around the nail. Wrap the other piece of wire around the penny. Stick the nail and one edge of the coin into the lemon.

Voila! You've just built a battery that could power a small lightbulb.

Seems easy, right? No big deal? That's because batteries and electricity are part of your everyday life.

But people were stunned when Italian scientist Alessandro Volta built the world's first battery in 1800. Using cardboard soaked in salt water and discs of zinc and copper, Volta produced a continuous stream of electric charges. It was a moment that changed the world.

You can also make a lemon battery using a zinc strip instead of a nail and a copper strip instead of a penny.

Q: Why did the scientist bury the battery?

A: It was dead.

19

Current Events

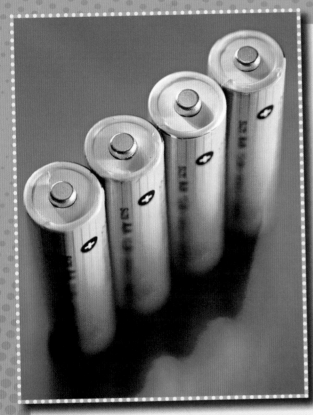

Why was Volta's experiment so important? Because he created a brand new kind of electricity. Today we call it current electricity.

What's so special about current electricity? It can be produced anytime, anywhere.

And that's not all. People can control how, when, and where it flows. That's pretty handy.

By 1900, companies in the United States were selling more than 2 million batteries every year. Today, that number has skyrocketed to 3 billion. It's hard to imagine what our lives would be like without batteries.

Q: Why do scientists study electricity?

A: To learn about current events.

Q: When does a battery go shopping?

A: When it's out of juice.

Mysterious Magnets

Okay, okay, enough about electricity. Sure, it's awesome and amazing. But it's not the only subject of this book. Believe it or not, magnetism is just as fascinating.

People living in Asia discovered the mysterious natural force more than two thousand years ago. In Magnesia, Turkey, people found rocks that could attract and cling to some metals. Today, we call anything that acts like those rocks a **magnet**.

People in China found the same "magical" rock. They noticed that when the rock floated in water or hung from a string, it slowly spun. It doesn't stop until one end points north and the other end points south. The Chinese couldn't explain the rock's strange behavior. But they used it to make the world's first magnetic compasses.

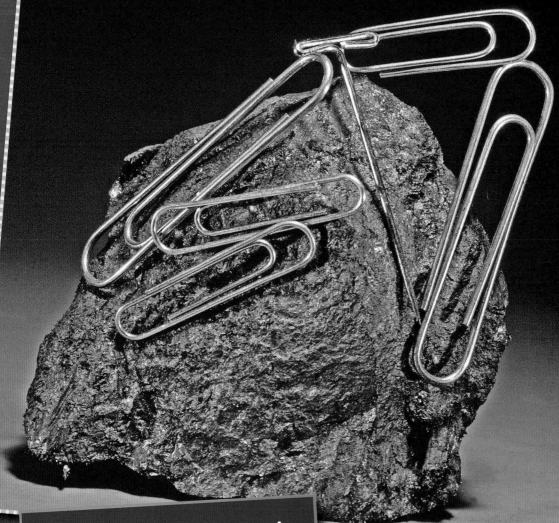

Q: How can you catch a dog by the tail?

A: Use a wag-net.

Solving the Mystery

11

Two thousand years is a long time. Really long. So you might not be surprised to hear that scientists now know tons more about how magnets work.

Do you know what they found? It turns out that magnetism and electricity have a whole lot in common. Believe it or not, whizzing, whirling, speeding, swirling electrons are the microscopic magic behind both electricity and magnetism.

All electrons move in two ways. They whiz around the **nucleus**. And they spin in circles. In most objects, half of the electrons in each atom spin one way, and half spin the other way. But in some objects, most of the electrons spin in the same direction. That **motion** makes the object magnetic.

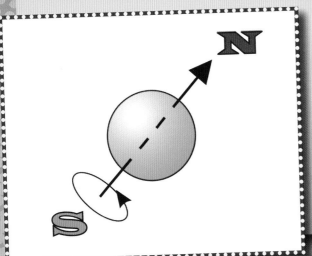

Q: What sport do the electrons inside magnets wish was part of the Olympics?

A: Synchronized spinning.

Q: What did one electron say to the other electron?

A: "Wanna go for a spin?"

12 More About Magnets

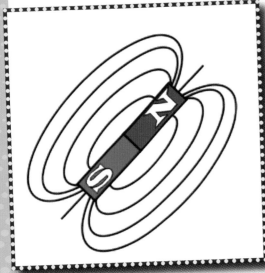

Do you know what else scientists have learned? Every magnet has a **magnetic field** around it. Inside that space, the magnet can attract metals like iron, nickel, and steel. The magnetic force is strongest close to the magnet. And it is weakest at the edges of the magnetic field.

Ever played with magnets like the ones on the next page? Guess what you would figure out? The magnetic field of one magnet can pull on (attract) or push against (repel) the magnetic field of another magnet. That's why the **north pole** of Magnet A sticks to the **south pole** of Magnet B. But it pushes away from the north pole of Magnet B.

Why do magnets act this way? They are trying to line up with both their magnetic fields pointing in the same direction.

Q: Where do magnets play baseball?

A: In a magnetic field.

Q: What's a magnet's favorite sport?

A: Pole vaulting.

13 A Magnetic World

Remember William Gilbert? He's the British scientist you read about on page 10.

Well, Gilbert didn't just study amber and static electricity. He was also interested in magnets. In fact, he wrote a famous book called *On the Magnet*.

Gilbert figured out why magnetic compasses work. It's because Earth is a giant magnet! Our planet's North Pole attracts one end of a compass's magnetic needle. And the South Pole attracts the other end. Earth's magnetic field extends way, way out into space.

And guess what! Some animals can feel Earth's magnetic field. Yup, it's true. Some birds, butterflies, fish, turtles, and whales use magnetism to find their way when they **migrate** from place to place.

Q: What did the compass say to Earth?

A: "You've got a magnetic personality."

Q: How do birds know when to migrate?

A: They watch the Feather Channel.

An Amazing Accident!

In 1820, Danish scientist Hans Christian Oersted proved just how much electricity and magnetism have in common. But it was by accident.

Oersted connected the ends of a wire to a battery. That meant electricity was flowing round and round a **circuit**.

Out of the corner of his eye, Oersted noticed something surprising. The magnetic needle on a nearby compass was moving. But why?

Oersted had an idea. He reconnected the wire to change the direction of the electric current. Guess what happened—the compass needle changed direction too. The electric current was creating a magnetic field around the wire. And the magnetic field was affecting the compass needle. Electricity could produce magnetism!

Q: How do you fix a short circuit?

A: Lengthen it.

It's easy to recreate Oersted's experiment. When you push down the lever to complete the circuit, you will see the needle on the compass move.

Q: What does an electric current have in common with a tightrope walker?

A: They both like to travel along

Easy On, Easy Off

Hans Christian Oersted had done more than discover **electromagnetism**. Much more. He'd given scientists the ability to create a powerful new tool—the **electromagnet**.

Why are electromagnets so much more useful than regular magnets? Because they can be turned on and off. That's right! A quick flip of a switch starts or stops the flow of electricity.

By 1832, American scientist Joseph Henry had built an electromagnet strong enough to lift 3,600 pounds (1,633 kilograms). That's about the weight of a small car.

Today electromagnets are used in everything from doorbells and electric guitars to junkyard cranes and high-speed trains. Life just wouldn't be the same without them.

Q: What did the wrecked car say to the electromagnet?

A: "Can I have a lift?"

Q: What did the doorbell say to the delivery man?

A: "Give me a ring some time."

16 Motors and Motion

But wait, that's not all. If it weren't for electromagnets, electric motors wouldn't exist. And electric motors are important. Really important. Electric motors power everything from vacuum cleaners and refrigerators to power tools and electric cars.

How do these motors work? They turn electrical energy into motion.

A motor consists of an iron shaft wrapped in a wire coil. As electric current travels through the wire, the shaft becomes an electromagnet. A second magnet surrounding the shaft causes the shaft to spin, and that keeps the motor running.

Some motors are as small as the head of a pin. Others are bigger than a tractor-trailer truck. But they all work the same way.

Q: Why did the oven and the dishwasher want to be more like the refrigerator?

A: Because it was so cool.

Q: What did the electromagnet say to the lost electron?

A: "Just go with the flow."

Power to the People

After Hans Christian Oersted made his incredible discovery, scientists began asking an important question: Can magnetism produce electricity?

You know what they discovered? It can. British scientist Michael Faraday proved it in 1831. All he had to do was move a magnet.

When Faraday pushed a magnet toward a coil of wire, electric current flowed in one direction. And when he pulled the magnet away from the wire, electricity flowed in the opposite direction.

Sounds simple, right? But it was an important discovery. Why? Because most modern power plants use magnets to make electricity. The current flows through power lines to our homes. It lights up lamps, toasts bread, charges cell phones, and much more. It's hard to imagine life without electricity—or magnetism.

Q: How did Michael Faraday pay for his magnets?

A: He charged them.

MASTER CHARGE

MICHAEL FARADAY

exp 1831

Q: Why did the people put sunflowers in their garden?

A: They wanted their own power plants.

How to Write Your Own Jokes

Writing jokes isn't hard if you keep three helpful hints in mind:

1. It's usually easier to think of a joke's punch line, or answer, first. Then work backward to come up with the setup, or question.

2. Keep the setup short and simple. People who listen to your joke will want to try to guess the answer. It's half the fun of hearing the joke. But if the question is too long, your listeners won't be able to remember it all. They'll feel frustrated instead of excited.

3. Keep the answer short and simple too. That way it will pack more of a punch.

Popular Expressions

Ever heard someone say: "I really look up to you"?
It means the person admires you.

Can you use this popular expression as the punch line for a joke? You bet!

When you look at a globe, we see the North Pole at the top and the South Pole at the bottom. So here's a question that works perfectly with your punch line:

Q: What did the South Pole say to the North Pole?

A: "I really look up to you."

Can you think of another joke that uses a popular expression as a punch line?

A homograph is a word with two or more different meanings. One example is the word *needles*. It can be used to describe the thin, flat leaves on evergreen trees or the movable pointer on a compass.

You can create a joke that plays with the two different meanings. Here's an example:

Q: **What do compasses have in common with pine trees?**

A: **They both have needles.**

Homophones are two or more words that sound the same, but are spelled differently and have different meanings. For example, the words *commotion* and *co-motion* are homophones.

You can create a great joke by mixing homophones. Here's an example:

Q: Why did the electric motors work together?

A: They wanted to make a co-motion.

These jokes are fun because your family and friends might be able to guess the answers. And sometimes they'll come up with different answers that are just as good. Then you'll have some brand-new jokes to tell someone else.

You can have lots of fun using homographs and homophones to create jokes that will amuse your friends.

Similar Sounds, Different Meanings

Changing a few little letters can also result in words that sound almost the same, like *lion* and *lying* or *cheetah* and *cheater*. And these word pairs can be the inspiration for some hilarious jokes.

Here's an example:

Q: Who's an electron's best friend?

A: Adam.

This joke works because the words "atom" and "Adam" sound similar.

Can you think of another joke that uses similar-sounding words to really pack a punch?

Rhyme Time

Playing with words to create rhymes can be highly entertaining. It's even better when a rhyme is the heart of a joke. Here's an example:

Q: How do scientists know where lightning will strike?

A: They look at a zap map.

Getting Silly

Sometimes the best jokes are ones that are just plain silly or ridiculous. Get ready to laugh out loud—here are some great examples:

Q: What do "amber" and "straw" have in common?

A: Both words have five letters.

Q: How is lightning different from the electricity in your home?

A: It's free.

Your Jokes in Print

Now it's your turn. See if you can come up with some seriously silly jokes of your own. Then share them with your family and friends.

You can submit your most science-sational jokes to: mas@melissa-stewart.com.
Be sure to include your first name and your age.

The best jokes will be posted on Fridays at: http://celebratescience.blogspot.com
People all over the world will be able to read and enjoy them. You can send drawings too. Now get to work on some jokes, and don't forget to have a good time!

Words to Know

atom—Tiny particle that makes up everything on Earth.

circuit—The path an electric current takes from a power source to the point of use.

electricity—Energy resulting from the flow of charged particles, such as electrons.

electromagnet—A device that is magnetized by an electric current.

electromagnetism—Magnetism produced by an electric current.

electron—A negatively charged particle that whizzes around the nucleus of an atom.

lightning—A stream of electricity that occurs during a thunderstorm. It occurs because positive and negative electrical charges separate inside the cloud.

magnet—An object or material that can attract certain substances, such as iron or steel.

magnetic field—The area around a magnet in which the magnetic force has the power to attract other objects or materials, especially those made of iron and steel.

magnetism—The attractive power of some objects and materials, especially the metals iron and steel.

migrate—To move from place to place.

motion—Movement.

neutron—A particle inside the nucleus of an atom. It has no charge.

north pole—One end of a bar magnet. The north pole of one magnet attracts the south pole of another magnet.

nucleus—The center of an atom. It consists of protons and neutrons.

proton—A positively-charged particle inside the nucleus of an atom.

resin—A thick, sticky liquid made by some trees, including pine trees.

south pole—One end of a bar magnet. The south pole of one magnet attracts the north pole of another magnet.

static electricity—The buildup of electric charges on a surface.

stun—To shock.

Learn More

Books

Gray, Susan Heinrichs. *Experiments with Electricity.* New York: Children's Press, 2011.

Hellweg, Paul. *The American Heritage Children's Thesaurus.* New York: Houghton Mifflin Harcourt, 2007.

Mullins, Matt. *Electricity.* New York: Children's Press, 2011.

Raum, Elizabeth. *What's the Attraction?: Magnetism.* Chicago: Heinemann-Raintree, 2007.

Wittells, Harriet and Joan Greisman. *The Clear and Simple Thesaurus Dictionary.* New York: Grosset & Dunlap, 2006.

Internet Addresses

Energy Kids
http://www.eia.gov/kids/energy.cfm?page=electricity_home-basics

KidsConnect.com: Electricity
http://www.kidskonnect.com/subject-index/15-science/72-electricity.html

Kids Science Experiments: Magnetism
http://www.kids-science-experiments.com/cat_magnetic.html

Index